by Shirley Frederick

HAMPTON-BROWN

These are the grasslands of South Dakota.

This is where the buffalo run.

This is the land of the Lakota people,

who dance to the beat of the drum.

Picture a world of blue sky and sunshine.

Here you can see the antelope run.

This is the world of the Lakota people,

who dance to the beat of the drum.

Picture a world of blooming flowers
that open each morning and reach for the sun.
This is the world of the Lakota people,
who dance to the beat of the drum.

Picture a world where eagles soar
and coyotes greet the moon with song.
This is the world of the Lakota people,
who live to the beat of the drum.

Many years ago, the Lakota people hunted the buffalo. They dried or stewed buffalo meat for food. They ate deer and antelope, too.

The Lakota lived in tepees made of buffalo hides. The people drew pictures on their tepees, so each one was different. When snow fell and cold winds blew, a fire inside the tepee kept everyone warm.

Buffalo hunters were very brave. A buffalo runs fast, and it has sharp horns. The hunters would ride close to a buffalo and shoot it with bow and arrows. Some strong hunters threw spears, too.

Before the hunt, the people did the buffalo dance. They sang songs and beat the drum and danced in the moonlight.

The world of the Lakota people is different today. The Lakota people get much of their food at stores now. The boys and girls ride a bus to school and study many new things. After school they still ride horses, and they still like to dance.

In this new world lives a
man named Dallas Chief Eagle, Jr.
He wants to share this world with the
children who live here and with the children
of the city.

When Chief Eagle was a child, he felt sad and
angry. After he grew up, he wanted to help children
be happy and strong, so he became a teacher. In his
school there are no desks or pencils or paper,
but there are plenty of children.

Chief Eagle explains that the hoop is
a circle. It is the circle of life. Each hoop
is perfect, just like the boy or
girl who holds it.

At the school today, Chief Eagle
is showing some boys and girls how
to dance. With two hoops each child
can be a tree—with three hoops,
a flower—with four hoops, an eagle.
Then the children dance in
a circle. No one is in front.
No one is in back. In the
circle, everyone is the same.

"The hoop is like a family," Chief Eagle says. "We all belong in the circle. Some of us are big, and some of us are little, but we can all help each other."

"A circle is like the seasons. The same seasons come every year. In the winter we stay inside and study. Spring is a time when life renews itself. In the summer we work hard. In the fall we dance for the people. Then winter returns, and we start the circle again."

Soon Chief Eagle begins to dance. He has hoops of many colors.

"The hoops are like the people of the world," he says. "We seem different, but inside we feel the same. We all feel happy. We all feel sad." As he moves, he spins the hoops around and around.

He adds more hoops and more. He spins and dances and adds more hoops. He spins the hoops and makes a world of many hoops, many people. What a picture he makes!

These are the grasslands of South Dakota.

This is the land where the buffalo run.

This is a world of many different children,

who dance together to the beat of the drum.